FORWARD

BACK

FORWARD

BACK

TURN 45°

PUSH
VACUUM

FORWARD

BACK

FORWARD

BACK

TURN 45°

© 2021 HOWTOVACUUM.COM

PUSH
VACUUM

FORWARD

BACK

FORWARD

BACK

VACUUM UNDER STUFF

PUSH VACUUM

FORWARD

BACK

FORWARD

BACK

TURN 45°

PUSH
VACUUM

FORWARD

BACK

FORWARD

BACK

VACUUM

UNDER

MORE

STUFF

PUSH
VACUUM

FORWARD

BACK

FORWARD

BACK

TURN 30°

PUSH
VACUUM

FORWARD

BACK

FORWARD

BACK

TURN 30°

PUSH
VACUUM

FORWARD

BACK

FORWARD

BACK

TURN VACUUM OFF

PUT VACUUM AWAY

www.ingramcontent.com/pod-product-compliance
Lightning Source LLC
Chambersburg PA
CBHW060918130726
48001CB00006B/2299